The Guessing Jar

by Margie Burton, Cathy French, and Tammy Jones

Table of Contents

Can We Guess How Many Crackers We Have?

Look at this guessing jar.

We are trying to guess how many crackers are in this jar.

What is your guess?

We counted the crackers.
There were three stacks of ten crackers and two left over.

There were 32 crackers in the jar.

Our teacher said there is a way to help us guess. He gave us a jar with a line on it. He put 25 crackers in the jar.

The crackers came up to the line. He said we can use the line to see that there are 25 crackers in the jar.

Then our teacher put some crackers in another jar. He told us to guess how many crackers he put in it.

We looked at the line on the first jar to help us guess.

What is your guess?

Did you guess less than 25? We did.

We counted the crackers in the other jar. There was one stack of ten crackers and six left over. There were 16 crackers in the jar.

Can We Guess How Many Cherries We Have?

Now look at these jars.
They have cherries in them.

The jar with the line on it
has 25 cherries in it.
How many cherries do you think
are in the other jar?
What is your guess?

Did you guess a number more than 25?
We did. We counted the cherries.
There were 5 groups of 10 cherries.

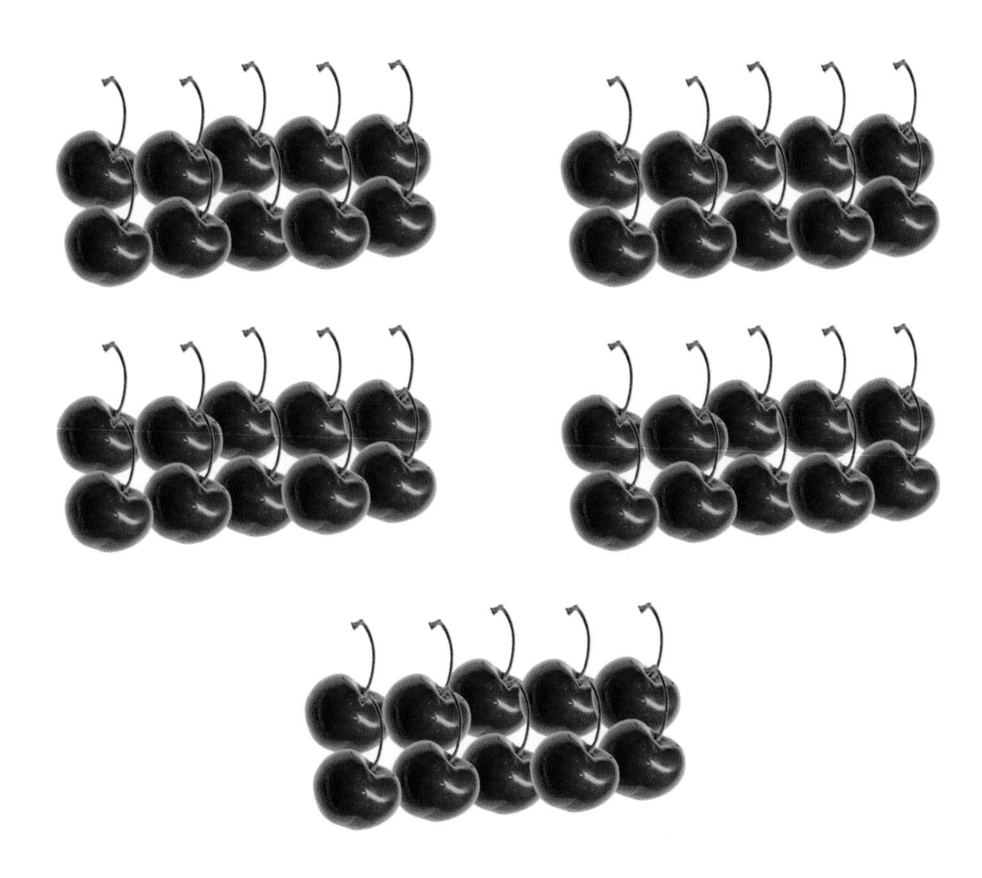

There were 50 cherries in the jar.

Can We Guess If Things Are Not the Same?

Now look at these jars.

The jar with the line on it has 60 marbles in it. The other jar has balls in it. How many balls do you think are in the jar? What is your guess?

Did you guess less than 60?
We did. We counted the balls.
There were 6 balls.

How did you do?

There are not as many balls
as marbles. The balls are bigger
than the marbles.

Look at the jars now.

The jar with the line on it has five cars in it.

The other jar has fish in it.

How many fish do you think are in the jar?

What is your guess?

Did you guess more than 5?
We did. We counted the fish.
There were 70 fish.

There are a lot more fish than cars.
The fish are smaller than the cars.

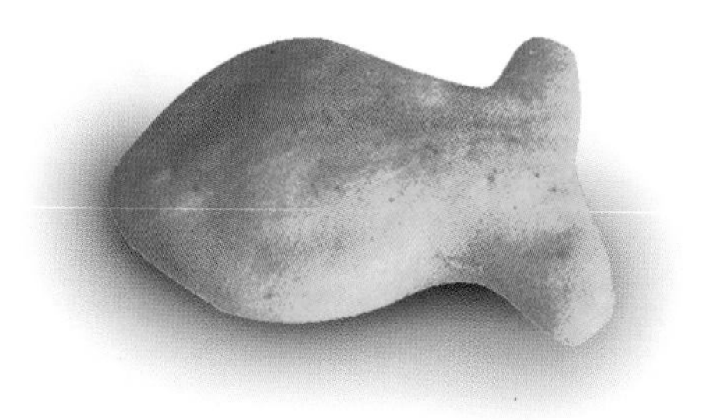

How did you do?

A guessing jar can be fun.